The Making of the Churchill Memorial Screen at St Paul's Cathedral

Gabrielle Ridler

Maytime Publishing

First Published in 2009 by
Maytime Publishing
Furze View
Timberscombe
Minehead
Somerset TA24 7TY

ISBN 978-0-9562728-0-5

Photographic Acknowledgments
All photography is by the author, unless otherwise indicated.

Design and Layout by
Terrence and Sally Clark
Wildfields Farm, Wood Street Village
Guildford, Surrey GU3 3BP

Printed in Great Britain

Photograph by Michael Ireland

Author's note

I was fortunate indeed to have been a member of the team making the Winston Churchill Memorial Screen for the Crypt of St Paul's Cathedral in 2004. Aware that not many people have much of an idea how such a large public work of art becomes a tangible, solid reality, I felt compelled to record the process, and to describe the work and life of the group of people who made it.

I would like to give heartfelt thanks to my editors Terry and Sally Clark for their expert work on the design and layout of this publication. My thanks also go to Dick Quinnell for proofreading and helpful comments; to Peter Parkinson for writing the foreword and providing a very useful glossary; to Bex Clark for making a special trip to photograph the screens at the Cathedral and the gate at the Victoria & Albert Museum, and to my dear husband Jim Horrobin for getting this marvellous job in the first place.

Gabrielle Horrobin
16 April 2008

Loon

Foreword

In the early nineteen eighties, as a college lecturer at West Surrey College of Art and Design in Farnham, I invited Jim Horrobin to visit the college to demonstrate blacksmithing skills and talk about his work to the students. Earlier that year the College had hosted a British Artist Blacksmiths Association Conference, and two eminent East European blacksmiths had been invited as guest demonstrators. They arrived with some fifty kilograms of excess baggage in the form of a large timber crate full of blacksmithing tools.

When Jim Horrobin arrived from Somerset a few months later, I met him at his car, and, expecting him to have brought a box of tools, asked if he needed help to carry them to the workshop. He looked slightly bemused at the question and climbed out of the driving seat, carrying just one hammer. With this, he kept the students spellbound for most of the day.

This small incident has stayed with me ever since, as a significant insight into an attitude of mind, and the character of the man whose work this book describes. It was a pivotal lesson for art students to appreciate that creativity is not dependent on a large collection of tools and equipment, but relies essentially on the judgement, skills and experience of an individual.

This book provides an intriguing insight into a world few people experience. Few today work in factories, manufacturing the multitude of products we use in our daily lives. Fewer still work in small workshops, as artist craftspeople designing and making special one-off pieces of work for a particular client or place. This book offers a glimpse of that world and the people who inhabit it.

Few projects are documented in this kind of detail. Part diary, part description, part working notes, it provides a fascinating insight into a year in the life of a group of people brought together by Jim and Gabrielle, to complete a large and challenging commission. It describes the complexity of the project and the range of specialist skills and creativity brought to bear - in a spirit of mutual respect - by individuals all working under the demanding but relaxed leadership of Jim Horrobin.

Peter Parkinson

April 2009

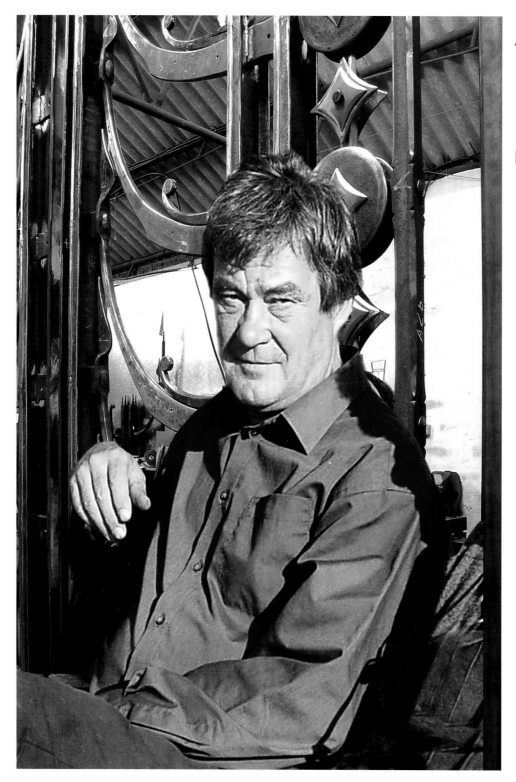

James Horrobin

Master Blacksmith

James Horrobin has been a blacksmith for over 40 years. He grew up on an RAF camp; his father Harry was Warrant Officer in charge of the gun repair workshops.
He remembers playing on the Bofors Guns while his bike was being repaired.
In 1961 his father retired from the Forces and bought a forge on Exmoor where Jim started work as his apprentice, aged 15. He always had a natural penchant for drawing, and enjoyed making small domestic objects and church work.

In 1978 the British Artist Blacksmiths Association (BABA) was founded, and in the following years together with the Crafts Council participated in a series of conferences and exhibitions which bought together both British and international artist blacksmiths. Jim was a founder member; it was a great education and changed the vocabulary of participating blacksmiths.

James uses traditional hand forging techniques combined with modern fabrication methods. He also takes advantage of new technology. CAD is used not as a design aid, but to ensure precision. His designs are contemporary; they have a natural organic feel inspired by his surroundings of sea and landscape. He uses both ferrous and non-ferrous metals, and experiments with surface texture and patination. He designs and manufactures architectural, ecclesiastic, domestic and sculptural metalwork to commission from his workshop and studio at Porlock. Samples of his work can be seen in many public places. Past commissions include: gates for the Metalwork Gallery at the V&A Museum, London; gates for Bishop Fox's Community School, Taunton, Somerset; lanterns for the portico of St Pauls' Chapel, Broadway, New York; gates to the summer garden at Antony House, Cornwall; the Churchill Memorial Screen, St Paul's Cathedral, London; a screen at Torre Abbey, Torquay, Devon.
James is a member of the Devon Guild of Craftsmen, and of BABA (British Artist Blacksmiths Association). He holds the Silver Medal of the Worshipful Company of Blacksmiths, and was given their Tonypandy Award for his work on the Churchill Memorial Screen at St Paul's Cathedral.
Comprehensive information and photographs of commissions can be seen at the website: www.doverhay.co.uk, also at the slide index of the Crafts Council: www.photostore.org.uk/home.aspx

Photograph by Bex Clark

This page, left to right:
Gates at the Victoria & Albert Museum
Whitehall railings
Balustrade for Saatchi residence.

Opposite left:
Portcullis at Whitehall

Top to bottom:
Walled Garden Gate
Anniversary Gate
Entrance Screen, 66 Cheapside EC2

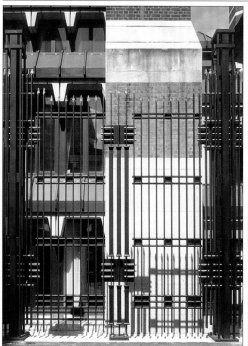

Sir Winston Churchill's State Funeral

The Winston Churchill Memorial Screen was specially commissioned by the Dean and Chapter of St Paul's Cathedral and designed and made by blacksmith James Horrobin and his team in 2004. The screen commemorates the third great national hero to have a State Funeral at the Cathedral, and stands as a memorial to Sir Winston Churchill in the Crypt, alongside those of the Duke of Wellington and Lord Nelson.

On the 30th of January 2005, just two months after the completion and installation of the Screen, Churchill's magnificent state funeral and memorial service was again shown on TV. Watching the programme on the 40th anniversary of that event gave us a deep sense of having taken part in history; in some measure validating all the attention to detail that had gone into our work on the Memorial Screen.

The insignia of the Knight of the Garter resting on Churchill's coffin were a reminder of the many honours he had received. We were fascinated to recognise members of the Churchill family, the Royal family, and other well known public figures, some of whom we had the privilege of meeting 40 years on at the dedication ceremony for the Screen, in the Crypt of St Paul's Cathedral.

Churchill's Funeral at St Paul's   ©©

 ## ST PAUL'S CATHEDRAL

The Deanery, 9 Amen Court, London EC4M 7BU

From The Dean of St Paul's
The Very Revd Dr John Moses

15 December 2004

James Horrobin Esq
Doverhay Forge Studios
Porlock
Minehead
Somerset TA24 8QB

Now that last Tuesday's ceremony is little more than a memory, may I write to thank you on behalf of all of us at St Paul's for all that you and your team have done in bringing the Churchill Gates to life. I cannot tell you how thrilled I am. They have fulfilled every expectation we had as a Chapter and are a very significant addition to the life of St Paul's. I know they have already given great delight to large numbers of people, including members of the Churchill family, and I shall be glad if you will convey to Gabrielle and all your team the great appreciation of every one of us.

With every best wish

 Telephone: 020 7236 2827
Email: thedean@stpaulscathedral.org.uk

Facsimile: 020 7332 0298
Website: www.stpauls.co.uk

INVESTOR IN PEOPLE

Letter from the
Dean of St Paul's Cathedral, the Very Reverend Dr John Moses

The Brief

In October 2001 Doverhay Forge Studios received an enquiry about a screen for St Paul's in memory of Sir Winston Churchill from Peter Burman, Director at the Centre for Conservation, University of York. We sent a brochure showing images of recent work and confirmed an interest in the project. On 14th March we had a reply, telling us that James Horrobin was not short listed for the commission.

The following August we were somewhat surprised to receive a letter from the Treasurer of St Paul's Cathedral, the Reverend Canon Philip Buckler. This informed us of the Dean and Chapter of St Paul's resolve, in consultation with the Churchill family, to commission a screen and set of gates to be positioned within the crypt of the Cathedral, as a permanent memorial to Sir Winston Churchill. James Horrobin and one other artist craftsman had been selected and invited to submit designs. The date for the submission of proposals was set for the 30 October 2002.

The project brief stated the purpose of the memorial:
to be a commemoration of the connection between Sir Winston and the Cathedral, embodied in his memorable message to the Lord Mayor of London during the Second World War: "At all costs St Paul's must be saved"; to perpetuate the memory of the many occasions when Sir Winston was present in St Paul's, and the fact that his own state funeral was here; to provide a focus for one of the greatest figures of the nation during the twentieth century; and by placing the memorial in the crypt, to provide a direct visual and symbolic link between the commemoration of the Duke of Wellington, the commemoration of Admiral Lord Nelson and the commemoration of Sir Winston. The memorial was to divide the commemorative area of the crypt from the area used for welcoming visitors and for providing services to them.

Important historical precedents for a screen or gates of metalwork were cited: the notable ironwork in the Cathedral by Jean Tijou; the celebrated wrought iron gates at Roskilde Cathedral in Denmark by Caspar Finke; the comparatively recent work such as the Bankside Gates at Shakespeare's Globe by Brian Russell for Richard Quinnell.

As a guide figure the total cost of the project was not to exceed £250,000

ST PAUL'S CATHEDRAL

'*At all costs
St Paul's must
be saved*'

Winston Churchill
29 December 1940

The Dedication Programme

Above from the left: Ged Kennett, Betsy Houlton, Jim Horrobin, Julian Fraser (at the back), Dot Kuzniar, Dom Hesp, Matt Horrobin, John Hesp, Charlie Hickman, Charles Braby, Gerald Gilbert, Alec Gannon

The Roadwater workshop Drawing by Julian Fraser

Photograph by Betsy Houlton

The Team

The Churchill Memorial Screen for St Paul's Cathedral has been the most interesting and challenging project Doverhay Forge Studios have undertaken, both in terms of collaboration with others, and in researching new techniques.

All team members were local craftspeople, many are friends.
Charlie Hickman, who transformed a barn into the workshop, helped Jim with much of the forge work, and carried out the finishing; Alec Gannon was in charge of installation. Gabrielle, Jim's wife (and the author of this record) looked after the office, designed the insignia roundels, and produced the presentation drawings. Jim's son Matt relocated from Seattle with his wife, two babies and dog; he developed patination techniques for all bronze components.
The brothers John and Dominic Hesp, both artists and expert metalworkers, have worked with us on many projects in the past. John was project manager and did all CAD drawings. He became a father for the first time before the job was finished. Together with Dom he designed the jigs, and the 'Trojan Horse' device. Their inventiveness and skill have been invaluable.
Phil Gannon - brother to Alec - a building surveyor, voluntarily surveyed the marking-out for drilling the piers for the top bearings. Betsy Houlton, an American we met at BABA's 25th anniversary celebrations, was here in training, to observe and learn.
The artist Julian Fraser whose pencil captured much of the action, Charles Braby, Dot Kuzniar, Ged Kennett, Ben Horrobin, Barron Tremaine, Gerald Gilbert, Mike Witney, Trevor and Steve at Devon Metalcrafts, and David Pankhurst for his work on the Memorial Plaque, have helped create this work. All are very proud to have worked on the project.

Below from left:
John and Dom thinking, Jim showing Charlie and Betsy how to forge on the power hammer, Julian drawing.

Photograph by Betsy Houlton

Design Development & Proposals

James Horrobin's first design proposal is dated 21st November 2002. It explained the development of ideas for the Churchill Memorial Screen, and comprised: Design drawings; Watercolour rendered design elevations; CAD drawings, e.g. site survey plan and elevations; Plan of ground plaque; Design elevation showing gates hinged against piers; Design perspective and full size detail. Presentation folder with a series of design development sketches.

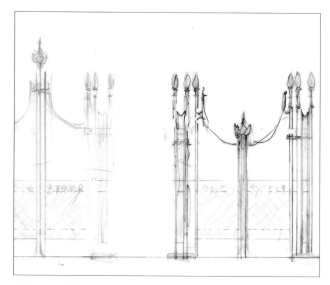

Above and below:
2 drawings showing how the design evolved

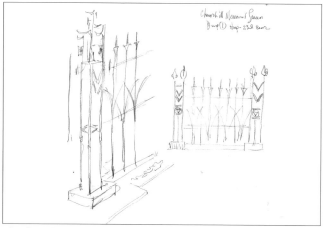

The first sketch by Jim Horrobin following the initial site visit

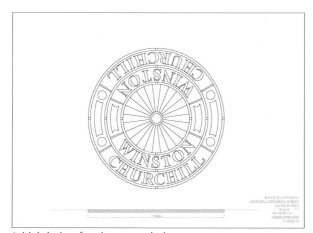

Initial design for the ground plaque
CAD drawing by John Hesp

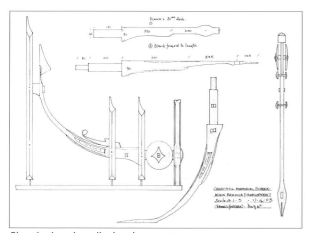

Sketch showing rib development

Design for heraldic roundel

Sketch design of components

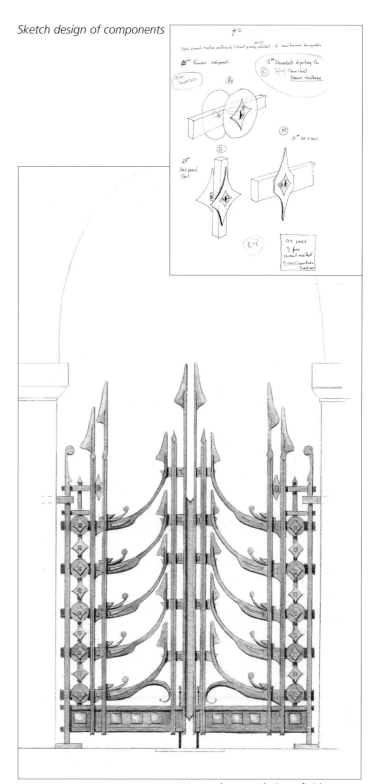

Watercolour rendering of side screen

CAD design perspective by John Hesp

The fully revised proposal is dated 19th September 2003 and was again presented with drawings, elevations and renderings, costings for the design development, and a statement by the artist.

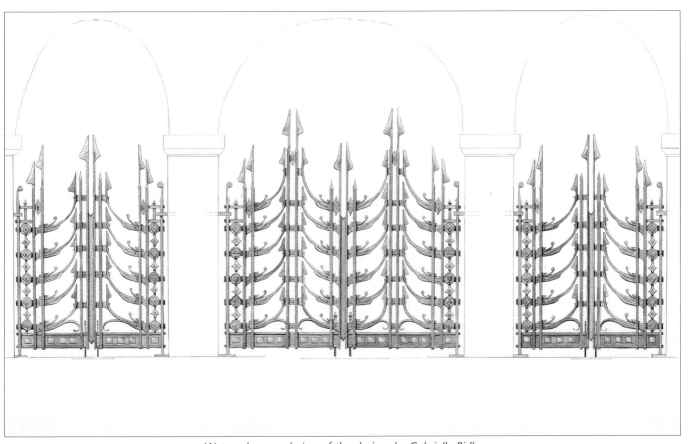

Watercolour rendering of the design, by Gabrielle Ridler

Photograph by Bex Clark

The Churchill Memorial Screen

Making the Memorial Screens

As our workshop at Porlock is rather quaint and small, a large enough venue had to be found to allow the making of the screens - with a height of 3.5m to the top of the flags of the centre screen and an overall width of 8m for all three screens; the side screens being 2m wide each and only slightly less high. A decision was made to use a large barn, and fit it out as a temporary workshop. First we had to turf out a great number of car wrecks, and a colourful assortment of farming paraphernalia. Then with the help of skilled team members, the huge space was sectioned off to accommodate a nearly sound-proofed grinding shop, a separate clean room for paint spraying; overhead lifting gear was installed; and very importantly, secure windows and doors. Tools, machinery, and the all-important kettle were in place, and making began in February 2004.

Traditionally a design is drawn up full size on boards. We jumped into the 21st century and put the whole design onto computer, with every part having a name and code.

Group 1 consisted of components that had to be hand forged, then linished and polished. In group 2 were components fabricated by engineering firms, all of which had to be cleaned up, filed, ground, welded or riveted on to the screen frame. Slam plates, lock assemblies and drop bolt assemblies also had to be sourced. Components for the assembly of frames were in group 3. Parts in group 4 were for the final assembly.

Jig frames were built, one for the side screen, another for the centre screen. All components were laid on the jigs and checked over and over again. The bottom truss was welded to the bottom rails and to the verticals. Verticals were welded to ribs and centre horizontals, centre horizontals riveted to ribs. Back stiles were riveted and rib wedges pinned. Finally all surface plates were fitted.

The screens contain patinated bronze details, face plates, bronze stars, buttons and flags, all together approximately 1200 small components.

We were given 12 months to complete the project. We received confirmation of the commission on November 22nd 2003, and we completed the installation on November 18th 2004.

Drawing of the barn workshop by Julian Fraser

Components

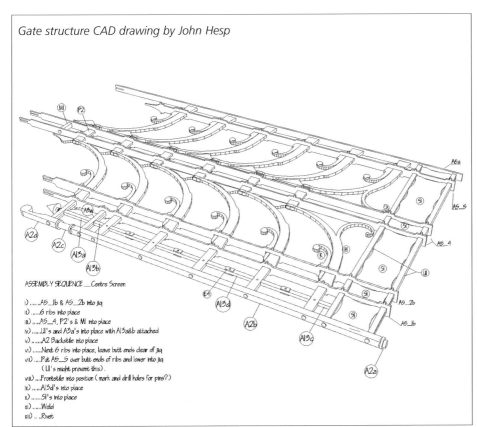

Gate structure CAD drawing by John Hesp

ASSEMBLY SEQUENCE __ Centre Screen

i) ......A5__1b & A5__2b into jig
ii) .....6 ribs into place
iii) .....A5__4, P2's & M1 into place
iv) .....U1's and A3a's into place with A13a&b attached
v) ......A2 Backstile into place
vi) ......Next 6 ribs into place, leave butt ends clear of jig
vii) ......Put A5__5 over butt ends of ribs and lower into jig
        (U1's might prevent this) .
viii) ....Frontstile into position (mark and drill holes for pins?)
ix) ......A13d's into place
x) ....51's into place
xi) ......Weld
xii) . ..Rivet

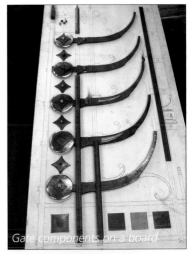
Gate components on a board

Gate components in boxes

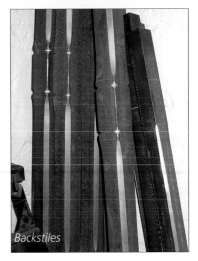
Backstiles

Branches

Jim's January Newsletter:

What is happening.
Thursday 5th January 2004

Present: Alec, John, Betsy, Charlie, Charles, Barron, Dom, Matt, Gabrielle, Jim, Ged.

Alec hauled over from Porlock most of the bits we need to make a start on the job. On Monday the laser cut verticals should be ready, so that Dom can start on the Main Frame jigs. There are some bits to finish on security of Charlie's farm barn. Charlie is arranging Public & Employer's liability insurance - to £2 million. (This means no one does anything they don't feel comfortable with).
Everyone should have their own subcontractor's insurance and licence to use any tool. Barron and Charles will run the grinding & finishing (final finish) shop and organise relays and equipment, so that no one gets too knocked out by it. Charlie will be finishing and spraying the balustrade over the next 2 weeks. Alec will organise a balustrade fixing team for early March - we hope.

Everyone should have their own personal tool-kit and safety gear; cost of consumables should be included in your quotes to the Company. All invoices for the supply of services and materials should be made out to Doverhay Forge Studios Ltd.

Matt will develop small components and run fire-scale and acid texture finishes. Betsy is going to develop surface textures. John has all the full dimension drawings available - please ask him for any you might need.

There are approx 1000 small components, 300 forged, 300 cast, 300 engineered, and maybe 500 larger heavy pieces. They are all dimensioned and have to fit both John's computer model and Dom's main frame jig.

Ged will develop patination of bronze components. Charlie has 44 ribs to forge. Jim has 44 rib flags to forge. Someone has 378 rivet heads to close up on 44 Face plates. Betsy has 240 rivets and drilling of square cover-plates to make.

Gabrielle will front the office and pay out the cheques. Jim will sweep up, make the tea and clean the toilets. The Churchill family want to make a visit to look at the work in April/May. Alec and John will liaise with the Trojan horse and trolleys. All spraying will be carried out after hours.

Matt is Health & Safety - no one works any machine unless instructed fully. Someone has to plant geraniums and Virginia creepers. Daily rota for washing up cups. All done by November 1st 2004. G and I are away last week of May - 1st week of June. All water, tea, juice, coffee - and cake for John at 3.30 - in stock.

Drawing by Julian Fraser

26

February - March 2004

Charlie's priorities at the beginning of February were still with our ongoing job, an oval staircase balustrade for a London residence.

He prepared the spray room and equipment - this was also groundwork for the Churchill Memorial Screens. He welded, ground and set the balustrade; spray painted it; and wrapped the panels ready for delivery. The balustrade was ready to be fixed in March.

At the same time work had begun on the St Paul's job. Rib jigs were made, one for bending the ribs, also one for drilling them. Grinding work was done in relays, engineering parts ordered.

Balustrade jig

Balustrade

Drawing by Julian Fraser

The Jigs

John Hesp had trained as a naval architect, and both he and his brother Dominic build boats. They have worked with us, together and separately, on many projects over the last 20 years or so.

The process of designing a jig is much more efficient with the use of computers. John has only one 3D master drawing of the screens on his computer. Any alterations are added to this drawing, and it has evolved with the necessary changes. The jig came from that drawing. Components for the jig were laser cut straight from the CAD drawings via email, and were of course perfect. In the past jigs were fabricated from stock metal, and total accuracy was not always possible. If mistakes were made they could multiply throughout and be very difficult to compensate for.

The components for the main frame of the screens are also laser cut, no forging or any other way of re-shaping was necessary, only grinding off and cleaning up. The jig consists of strips of metal which are welded together to form a grid which allows the main frame of the screens to be assembled on it with total accuracy. The CAD programme subtracts the shapes for the screen from the shapes needed for the strips, which creates strips with slots in the right place, and this is the Jig.

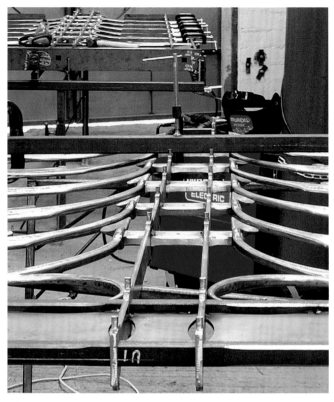

The Churchill Lion

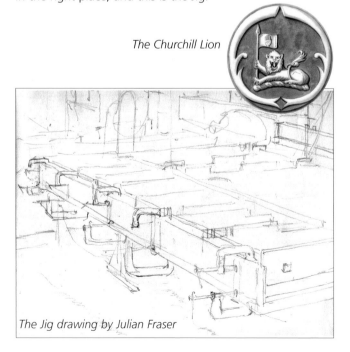

The Jig drawing by Julian Fraser

The Heraldic Roundels

The job of researching the life of Churchill, and to produce design drawings for roundels with images from his life, was my task. From the enormous choice of motifs that offered themselves from this extraordinary life, six were chosen.

*The Churchill Lion
*Date of Birth 1874
*Date of State Funeral at St Paul's Cathedral 1965
*The Breast Badge of the Knights of the Garter (1953)
*The Order of Merit (1946)
*The Shield of Cinque Ports (Warden of the Cinque Ports)

Treatment of the roundels is generally reminiscent of naval signalling flags. All bronze detail is polished and patinated. The material will darken in the recesses, but since they are all surface plates, will develop a mixed patina over time.

Pattern Making and Casting

We had approached several casting firms, made factory visits, discussed different methods of production and researched costings. Finally a local firm: Devon Metalcraft at Exmouth got the job. The pattern-maker chosen for the work, Gerald Gilbert - also a local, based at Wellington - had been working with Devon Metalcraft for some time.

Gerald is a jeweller and model maker by trade and works in a tiny workshop overlooking his back garden. Some of his creations can be seen up on the shelves, alongside a colourful array of photos, drawings and art posters. Using my line drawings, he made patterns from brass, copper and Milliput, a 2-pack plastic modelling compound. These patterns were delivered to Devon Metalcraft in Exmouth, where all components were cast in bronze. Subsequently the castings were returned to the pattern maker, who would refine detail and polish surfaces. Studs for riveting were then soldered individually to the back of each cast component, to allow castings to be attached to the textured, patinated roundels.

Gerald Gilbert's workshop

Roundels top to bottom:
The Churchill Lion
Order of Merit
Knight of the Garter
Cinque Ports

Newsletter April 2004

HMS Churchill
The voyage is well under way. No sight of land as yet, but favourable trade winds are speeding progress. All basic victuals are on board. Ribs are forged and all bending is done now. 60 Truss plates, 160 studs, 88 daggers and 25 top gallants are in progress and looking good. All being well, the first mainsail is ready to be raised, so I reckon we should have a picnic on Friday (30th April) afternoon at about 4pm. John, Dom, Matt, Charlie, Alec, Dot, Betsy, Charles, Ged, Gabrielle, Julian, Barron, Ben, Jo, together with all families are cordially invited by Cap'n Jim!

Captain Jim

The Dean's Visit – 24th May 2004

The prospect of this grand occasion was the cause of a much-needed spring clean on all fronts. The showroom at Porlock received particular attention, as it was to be the starting point of the visit. Elsewhere there was great sweeping and tidying till all was shipshape and the work completed to date could be shown to the best advantage.

Monday 24th May was a perfectly glorious Spring day. The Dean of St Paul's, The Very Reverend Dr John Moses, had been met at Taunton Station by Martin Stancliffe, Surveyor to the Fabric of St Paul's, and his wife Sarah, and driven to Doverhay Forge at Porlock. The first question the Dean had for Jim was: "Are you enjoying this work?" We could all honestly answer this with: "Yes, very much so".

The visitors were able to examine pattern samples and components of the heraldic roundels, look at plans and drawings of the Ground Memorial Plaque and a sample letter C in stainless steel set into a disc of naval brass. Following a demonstration of forging and chamfering bronze stars by Betsy and Dot, and a good look round our picturesque yard, our guests continued on to the other workshop. I quickly collected pre-ordered pasties and sandwiches from our local bakery, loaded up the car with all the fixings for a picnic - including tablecloth - and followed on. The boys had been briefed to clear a table space for this lunch party.

Now came the most important part of the visit: our client's first look at the actual screens. After months of seeing it two-dimensionally on plans, renderings and CAD perspective drawings, the Dean and Martin Stancliffe could see the real thing, and spend time walking round and examining the fully erected screen frames from every angle and side. Jim explained how the work would progress from here, showed how the additional components would enhance, deepen and add to the substance of the screens. Matt, Charlie and Alec demonstrated the function of the 'Trojan Horse', a device designed and built by John and Dom Hesp to transport, lift and erect the gates.

Just before it was time to drive the Dean back to catch his London train we invited him to walk up a small hill behind the workshop, to look at things from above.

From the left: Matt Horrobin, Martin Stancliffe, Dr John Moses, Dean of St Paul's Cathedral; Gabrielle Horrobin, Jim Horrobin, Charlie Hickman, Alec Gannon

Right: Martin Stancliffe, Jim Horrobin, Dr John Moses, Betsy Houlton

The workshop from above. Photograph by John Hesp

The "Trojan Horse" Device

Alec Gannon was in charge of installing the gates. As the doors at the Cathedral are just under 2m high and the gates measure 3.5m in height, the gate leaves had to be brought in on their pallet lying on edge, and then lifted into the upright.

The original idea to lift the gates off the trolley and the right way up was to use two small crane devices. This was not deemed ideal as it would have been a slow process, and not altogether safe - there could have been danger of dropping a gate.

John thought it should be easy to make something to do the job better. He chatted with Alec and Dom about it and together they came up with a plan. Dom had the idea how to make it, John produced a drawing on CAD, then Dom put it together with help from the team.

The 'Horse' consists of a frame on wheels, housing two scissor jacks, with a pivot on top of the jacks. The device is wheeled over a gate leaf, a 30mm dia pivot pin is inserted, the jacks lift the gate and the pivots rotate it till it is the right way up, then allow it to be dropped into place - ready to be hung from the journals.

The device has already proven extremely useful during making - the gates could be moved about freely – and it allowed a complete practice run of the fixing method.

Photograph by John Hesp

Drawings by Julian Fraser

The Ground Plaque

Jim and I paid a visit to the factory of the Pankhurst Tool & Die Company at Littleham near Exmouth, on a blazing day in June. We had a long and interesting talk with the managing director, David Pankhurst, were given a guided tour of the factory and talked with a dedicated team of workers. We also managed to have a mini holiday later on that lovely hot afternoon - headed down the coast to Budleigh Salterton and had our first, breathtakingly cold, swim of the year in the sea.

The ground plaque, set in the floor of the Crypt in the centre of the screen, is of naval brass, with inserted stainless steel lettering. It was manufactured by the method of wire erosion.

Very thin (10,000th inch dia) brass wire has an electric current passing through it. This creates a minute spark that erodes the metal in its path - where it is programmed to cut. In order to accommodate the size of the plaque (1.240m dia) Pankhurst's took the opportunity to install a brand new machine. John Hesp provided CAD drawings on CD. The final and approved lettering design is by Richard Kindersley.

The plaque was machined by the beginning of August. It was then assembled and the disc face polished before final assembly with the stainless steel letters. All was safely delivered to us by the end of September.

Top left: Spark Erosion Machine

Left: Ground Plaque

Phase II of making the Churchill Memorial Screens

Phase I was completed by the end of May. It had seen the manufacture of backstiles: chamfered, ground and linished to pre-finish; welded up, drilling holes marked out, drilled out and countersunk; de-greased ready for assembly in jig. Short top horizontals; vertical supports; vertical front stiles; ribs; short verticals; horizontals; rib wedges; truss plates; bottom horizontals were completed. All 6 screens were assembled. John rationalised slam plates, drop bolt and locking drawings.

By June Phase II was under way and would see all face plates, and complete sets of side panel roundels, decorative M12 bolts, spacers, and large bronze stars forged, ground and linished, and screwed to gate frame. Jim forged all top flags, and made 6 patterns for cast naval brass studs. Matt and Charlie ground and linished to 120 grit, drilled and fitted flags to verticals. Matt polished and patinated all bronze components.
Jim and Matt finished forging vertical face plates by Thursday 22 June. Matt arranged to pick these up with a trailer on Friday. Matt and Charlie straightened and ground edges only. John marked out groove end positions. Ben was set up with a bench at the gas forge - to make 400mm grooves. Matt forged short face plates.

John Hesp fitting slam plate

Drawing by Julian Fraser

Matt and Jim Horrobin forging vertical faceplates

June Visitors

Dick Quinnell, a long time friend, and founder of the British Artist Blacksmiths Association (BABA) and his wife Pauline came to stay, together with another fellow artist blacksmith, Peter Parkinson.
On that weekend in Mid June they visited both workshops, and had a good look at what we were up to. Their reaction was very positive. By then all three gate frames were complete, and the team was making great progress.

Dick Quinnell checking the screen

Betsy Houlton, Peter Parkinson, Pauline Quinnell, Jim Horrobin, Dick Quinnell, Charlie Hickman.

Progress of work during June and July

A number of other jobs were still in progress at that time. Jim finished forging components for a garden bench for an old customer; brackets were needed for lamps over the oval stair balustrade; a new technique was developed for a sculptural fireplace.

A meeting was set to discuss patinating. Betsy worked with Dot on side panel stars. A programme was set up for ground box & plate manufacture. Charlie researched soft grit-blast materials and equipment, and sprayed all jigs.
John drew up rib face plate rivets for engineer Mike Witney. Matt worked on vertical face plates. Charles finished all vertical face plates to 80 grit. Jim ordered the steel.
I checked on progress of the roundels, monitored all the above and dealt with correspondence and finances.
In early July Charlie designed and made the face plate straightener from a section of 'I' beam. Face plates were now ready for the centre groove to be cut on the fly press. The face plate top finials were cut. John had also sorted out the drilling jig for vertical face plates. Ged bandsawed out the rib face plates - known as 'daggers' because of their shape. Mike Whitney turned the 44 dagger and 80 stud rivets, as well as 4 top side panel horizontal bosses. Matt drilled 384 holes into the bottom truss face plates and then fitted 60 bronze plates with 240 brass countersunk rivets.
The project now went into a phase where the number of components increased. The end of July was completion target for all 1200 small components ready for finishing and fitting.
I sent image material to St Paul's for the Press office and paid everyone when I received the bills. Betsy had planished 30 side panel stars. John was thinking of Falmouth, and sailing his 27ft gaff-rigged cutter, the 'Hope'.
Alec had drawn up the ground journals and then went off to spend 4 weeks cycling from Bilbao to Faro. Charles also went on holiday and linked up with Alec in Spain for a week's cycling. Jim and Gabrielle had a family wedding at the end of July, and Charlie needed to get his hay in. So a bit of holiday was needed all round.

Exmoor gate

August 4th

Despite a somewhat reduced workforce the work progressed apace. August saw the completion of the heraldic roundels. All castings had been completed by Trevor and Steve at Devon Metalcraft. Detail was refined, lions, shields and badges polished, roundel edges finished and rivets attached by Gerald Gilbert the patternmaker. All was checked and collected by myself; I then had the job of marking the roundels for drilling.

Drawing by Julian Fraser

Fireplace slab

Bench

Gate Components

Gerald Gilbert's patternmaking

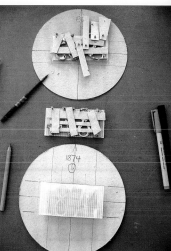

Progress through September

On 14th September we received the official invitation letter from the Dean for the Dedication Ceremony. From then on there was a busy exchange of emails and letters, with photos and information about the job and the team. St Paul's were planning a publication for the occasion; I liaised with the Press Office via email, and supplied drawings and images to Bill Henderson, the Graphic Designer in charge.

Plans for transporting the screens to London were now finalised. By early October Charlie had created a huge, enclosed area at the workshop. Protected like a space-man by white overalls and full face mask he proceeded to shotblast each screen, then went on to spray the screens with clear lacquer.

Alec and Phil Gannon were on site at St Paul's on the 7th October, to survey and measure. The Cathedral workforce would do the preparatory work, and dig out for hinge boxes & the ground plaque.

I finished designing and printing the invitations, maps and envelopes for our celebratory picnic on Friday 5th November, and started a to-do list and menu.

Preparations also included baking some cookies in the shape of roundel stars. The guest list was now up to 47 – all the people (and their partners) who had worked on the screens, and a few friends and family were invited.

Patinating

Wrapped and ready to go

Patinating and assembly, October

Jim had driven off to the other workshop, car laden with many boxes of finished bronze components: buttons, large stars, rib bolt heads, spacers, side panel stars, truss plate covers, and top flags.

Here at Doverhay Forge Matt is operating in his capacity as 'the Chemist', slaving over his plastic containers of acids and patinating potions. He has completed all the heraldic insignia components this morning: the garter star, order of merit, and all numerals; patinated the brassy flag of the Churchill lion, and the Cinque Ports shield to match the patina of the bronze.

This afternoon he is working on the naval brass slam plates. Only yesterday these had been finished by Jim: chamfered, linished and smoothed flat. After the acid bath – where they are watched carefully, only left until the colour looks exactly right – the slam plates are again rinsed off under running water. The metal is then dried off in ground maize meal. Another rub down with Scotch-Brite™ (and until then only touched by rubber-gloved fingers) and the patinated metal is heated till nearly too hot to touch. Then Briwax is brushed on, and when cooled, finished off with a good buffing.

John, Alec and Charlie had now set up all the screens. Matt, Jim and Charlie proceeded to rivet on all bronze detail. The heraldic roundels were fitted. A sub-frame for transporting the ground plaque was made by John and Alec. They also completed drop bolts & holders, made the ground box cover plates, and fitted slam plates and locks.

Meanwhile the second team went to St Paul's on a site visit, to pre-fix the top hinges and all ground journals. They finished by 11pm and came on home the same day. One of my tasks was to organise the engraving of a brass plaque with the names of all the team, to be fixed over one of the ground boxes at the foot of one of the side screens.

Loading and Fixing

Friday the 12th November. Charlie, Matt and Jim were busy getting everything ready for the Sculpture remover to load and transport the work to St Paul's. John was not with us that afternoon - he was very busy becoming a father for the first time. Baby Jack, practically our project baby, was born in the evening of November 12th.

On Monday 15th November the screens were loaded. All six gate leaves on their separate trolleys had been wheeled out of the workshop and on to the ramp of the van. When this was raised each trolley was carefully turned and parked in its allotted space - as shown on John's plan. Alec, Matt, Charlie, Jim - and new dad John, were busy slotting in the all-important 'Trojan Horse' devices, strapping down gates on trolleys, packing crates of components and tools, and making all secure. It was decided to take the fully laden van down the lane for a test drive, a nervous John riding in the back making sure nothing moved. But his meticulous planning paid off: all was well. Only a rear mudguard was broken, reversing back up - the recent heavy rain had created more bumps and potholes than ever in the lane. Finally all the bustle died down, people stood tiredly around. The last boxes of tools and gear were stowed. The empty workshop felt strange, and quite sad in its bareness, a few remnants of balloons from the party still dangling from the rafters. (About a week later a tractor was again parked in the barn, and made it seem less bare)

Above: The screens on trolleys
Below: Name plaque

MADE BY: James Horrobin, Gabrielle Ridler, Matt Horrobin, Charlie Hickman, John Hesp, Alec Gannon, Dominic Hesp, Charles Braby, Ged Kennett, Betsy Houlton, Dot Kuzniar, Devon Metalcraft, Pankhurst Tool & Die Co., Mike Witney, Gerald Gilbert, Ben Horrobin. 2004

Loading the screens

Fixing Day 1: Tuesday 16th November

The fixing team left early Tuesday morning, for London and St Paul's. Driving in via Ave Maria Lane, the van arrived at the entrance to the Cathedral service area.

Each horizontally-secured screen leaf on its individual trolley was unloaded, rolled down the ramp and into the Crypt. Here each trolley was reversed into the 'Trojan Horse' device, with the help of pivot pin and jacks lifted into position in the upright, and the leaf hung from the pre-fixed journals.

The Cathedral work crew had drilled the holes to receive the ground bolts. All this activity was being carefully hidden from public gaze. Shrouded panels were moved into place as soon as work ceased for a minute, and sheets draped over the screens, to obscure any glimpse of the newly erected Memorial Screen. All work and noise had to come to a halt on several occasions, when afternoon services were held in the cathedral above, and once to allow a reception to take place in the visitor area of the Crypt, following a commemorative service. By the evening both the Centre and the South Screen were up.

Fixing the screens

Photographs by Betsy Houlton

Using the 'Trojan Horse'

Ground Plaque

Fixing the Ground Plaque

Alec takes up the story:

"The ground plaque was fixed to a sub-frame which incorporated levelling screws (for bringing the plaque flush with the floor) and lugs for bolting down to the concrete sub-floor.

After we were confident of the level, we placed large dabs of resin adhesive on the concrete sub floor, where the levelling bolts would make contact, and lowered the plaque for the final time".

Fixing Day 2: Wednesday 17th November

This is when the second wave of fixers set out: Jim and Matt drove up to London - John and Dom decided they would not be needed - and arrived about 2 pm, just in time to see all three screens up. Although the work to finish and complete everything did take a bit more effort, everything was done by 11pm. Unfortunately the tired workers could not foresee the effects of numerous diversions and road works at that time of night: the drive home, usually an easy three hour trip, took them nearly twice as long; they didn't get back till after 4am.

The following day was spent unloading, tidying away, chatting, de-briefing. Meanwhile I had been busy working on the layout and setting up of a website, with some help. A last flurry of emails and photos were sent off to the press office at St Paul's. There were train tickets to organise; hotel bookings to be made; invitations to the dedication service to chase up - all team members were to receive one; end of month jobs in the office to finish; a new business card to design and get printed; and of course my posh frock to get, for this important occasion.

Jim Horrobin and the Dean looking through the screen to Nelson's tomb

The Press Conference

On Sunday evening, the 28th, Jim and I took the train to London. Next day a taxi took us to St Paul's, and we made our way to the Chapter House for the Press Conference at 2pm.

Statements were read by the Dean of St Paul's, The Very Reverend Dr John Moses; the Surveyor to the Fabric of St Paul's, Martin Stancliffe; and James Horrobin.

The members of the press - the Times, Guardian, Independent, Telegraph, Scotsman, BBC News etc. were represented and started to look a bit bored when Jim talked about the people on the team. There was a lot more interest in his father Harry having served in the RAF, regardless of the fact that he was now a total pacifist. The correspondent from the Times was particularly interested in how funding for the project was obtained. The reporter from the Guardian quoted Jim's words: "I hope the screen is perceived as a celebration of peace brought about by Mr Churchill's efforts".

A photo shoot followed at the Crypt: Jim and the Dean stood between the half-opened centre gates of the Churchill Memorial Screen, the ground plaque in the foreground, with photographers milling around. I kept quietly in the background, and snapped away with my own pimple of a camera - I knew I would not easily get another chance. This was my first look at the screens in situ; even though I had lived with them, and watched them grow for more than a year, it took my breath away.

The following morning we dressed in our finery and made our way to the Cathedral. Gradually other people from our team started to appear. We watched Lady Soames arrive, then Lady Thatcher, and many other large cars bearing dignitaries.

The Dedication

On 30th November 2004, the 130th anniversary of Churchill's birth, the Dedication and Installation of the Churchill Memorial Screen took place in the Crypt of St Paul's Cathedral; with trumpets sounding and the Cathedral choir singing; in the presence of HRH the Duke of Kent; the Dean and Chapter of St Paul's; Lady Mary Soames, daughter of Sir Winston, and other members of the Churchill Family; Sir Edward Heath, Lady Thatcher, Dame Jennifer Jenkins, Lord and Lady Howe; many other notable figures, and a bunch of metalwork folk from West Somerset.

Guests were seated on both sides of the screen, facing toward it: on one side the Churchill Family, specially invited dignitaries and the Dean and Chapter; on the other the parliamentarians, sponsors, and we craftsmen. Jim and I were shown to our reserved places beside Martin Stancliffe, Surveyor to the Fabric. The Installation and Dedication was led by the Dean and HRH the Duke of Kent. All joined in to sing the Hymn, with words by John Bunyan: 'He who would valiant be'. The reading was from Psalm 18. A new composition by Malcolm Archer, organist of St Paul's, was performed, a motet specially written for this commemorative ceremony, set to Winston Churchill's own words:
'In war: resolution. In defeat: defiance. In victory: magnanimity. In peace: goodwill.'
To emphasise Churchill's links with America, the 'Battle Hymn of the Republic' was included in this service, as it had been in his funeral service 40 years before.

The Dedication concluded with the National Anthem. After that everyone came forward, had a good and close look at the screens, and moved on to a reception at the west end of the crypt, where champagne and nibbles were served. Jim was introduced to HRH the Duke of Kent, shook hands with and chatted to Lady Soames, Lady Sandys and other members of the Churchill Family. He talked to Sir Edward Heath about his childhood on an RAF camp and conversed briefly with a frail Margaret Thatcher.

Guardian press cutting

National news

Churchill's life honoured in St Paul's ceremony

Lady Thatcher and Michael Howard at yesterday's dedication ceremony
Photograph: Chris Young/PA

John Ezard

The destiny of those few figures who save the sum of things — life, freedom, humane values or material prosperity — for posterity is to be half-forgotten by much of posterity, except in classroom history lessons.

It happened to Nelson and Wellington and it is happening to Sir Winston Churchill, who was honoured next to their tombs in St Paul's cathedral yesterday.

Churchill is part of the living memory of only a few of those who watched in the cathedral churchyard yesterday as groups of elderly VIPs filed down to the crypt for the dedication of a screen and gates in his memory.

The spectators, surrounded by lavish shops whose prices most of them could not afford,

were basking in the "broad, sunlit uplands" of prosperity which Churchill once promised if only we braced ourselves to win the war against Hitler. Yet there was puzzlement on their faces.

To remember the cathedral's last service in Churchill's honour — his funeral — you would have to be over 40. To have any clear memory of his speeches and broadcasts in the early 40s — or the desperate war which gave rise to them — you would need to be in your 70s.

So Sir Edward Heath, 88, a soldier mentioned in dispatches during the second world war and a junior whip in Churchill's last administration in the early 50s, was there, in a wheelchair.

So was a frail, slow-walking Lady Thatcher, 79, a Grantham schoolgirl during the war, who entered the crypt

supported on an escort's arm. Michael Howard — a stripling at 63 — was present representing the Conservative party.

Also in the congregation was Dame Jennifer Jenkins, whose late husband, the former Labour minister Roy Jenkins, called Churchill, "the greatest human being ever to occupy 10 Downing Street".

Yesterday a survey among history and politics academics rated him as the second most effective 20th century prime minister after Clement Attlee.

But the most senior current Labour MP present was the Frank Field. The most senior member of the royal family was the Queen's cousin, the Duke of Kent.

The Duke dedicated the screen to God "in proud and grateful remembrance of thy servant Winston

Leonard Spencer Churchill".

The dean of St Paul's, Dr John Moses, called Churchill "one of our nation's greatest servants".

The hymns were two of Churchill's favourites, Bunyan's To be a Pilgrim and the Battle Hymn of the Republic.

A specially composed choral piece by the cathedral's organist, Malcolm Archer, mixed Churchill's words with the trumpet blasts of the Last Post and Reveille.

For a moment they turned the ceremony into a rite for all the second world war's millions of dead.

guardian.co.uk/secondworldwar

The Churchill Memorial Screen

GLOSSARY

backstile - The heavy upright framing bar of a gate, on which it hinges.

CAD - Computer Aided Design. Drawings produced on a computer.

chamfer - A bevelled edge used both in woodwork and metalwork to remove the sharpness of a square corner.

chamfering - Hammering, grinding or filing a bevelled edge along a bar.

drop bolts - The vertical sliding bolts with handles which fit into sockets in the floor, to secure a gate in an open or closed position.

front stile - The vertical framing bar of a gate at the opposite side to the backstile. Locks and latches are normally fitted to the front stile.

80 grit - This number indicates the size of the grit used on abrasive paper or cloth. 80 grit means that the abrasive will pass through a sieve which has 80 holes per square inch. The larger the number, the finer the abrasive.

journal - An engineering term for a particular type of bearing. In these gates part of the backstile is machined near the top, to form a short circular shaft, allowing the backstile to rotate between split bearings secured to the masonry piers, forming a hinge.

ground journal - A short shaft machined at the very bottom of the backstile of a gate, designed to pivot in a bearing secured in the floor.

laser cutting - Cutting metal using a high powered laser, controlled by a computer.

leaf - One of a pair of gates.

linished - A linisher is a machine which uses an abrasive belt or disc, to smooth or shape metal.

patination - Patination is the coloured surface produced on metals by chemical treatments.

pattern - The hand made master form used to produce the mould for casting metal.

piers - The pillars to which in this case the gates are hinged.

slam plate - A narrow projecting plate fitted to the front stile of a gate. One of a pair of gates is normally secured shut, by a drop bolt locking into the ground socket. The second leaf then stops against the slam plate of the first. A lock or bolt secures the two gate leaves together.

Scotch-Brite™ - A proprietary fibrous abrasive pad, used to provide a semi-matt finish on metals.

PP 2009